A DVD-based study series
Study Guide

# THE DAWNING

*Christianity in the Roman Empire*

With Joe Stowell

A DVD-based study series
Study Guide

# THE DAWNING

*Christianity in the Roman Empire*

With Joe Stowell

Fifteen Lessons for Group Exploration

*Feeding the Soul with the Word of God*

The DayLight Bible Studies are based on programs produced by *Day of Discovery,* a Bible-teaching TV series of RBC Ministries.

© 2013 by Discovery House Publishers

Discovery House Publishers is affiliated with RBC Ministries,
Grand Rapids, Michigan.

Requests for permission to quote from this book should be directed to:

Permissions Department
Discovery House Publishers
P.O. Box 3566
Grand Rapids, MI 49501
Or contact us by e-mail at permissionsdept@dhp.org

All Scripture quotations, unless otherwise indicated, are taken from the
HOLY BIBLE, NEW INTERNATIONAL VERSION®, NIV®
Copyright © 1973, 1978, 1984 by Biblica, Inc. ™
Used by permission of Zondervan.
All rights reserved worldwide.
www.zondervan.com

Study questions by Andrew Sloan
Interior design by Sherri L. Hoffman
Cover design by Jeremy Culp
Cover photo by stock.xchng

**ISBN: 978-1-57293-775-8**

*Printed in the United States of America*

First Printing 2013

# CONTENTS

**INTRODUCTION**
An Unexpected Transformation — 7

**SESSION 1**
Rome: Ruler of the World — 9

**SESSION 2**
Rumors of a Better King — 17

**SESSION 3**
Rome Resists the Gospel — 25

**SESSION 4**
The Ways of Jesus — 33

**SESSION 5**
Persecution of Christians — 41

**SESSION 6**
The Marginalization of Christians — 49

**SESSION 7**
The Gospel: A Traveling Enterprise — 57

**SESSION 8**
Lessons from Capernaum — 65

**SESSION 9**
The Example of Peter — 73

**SESSION 10**
Ephesus: Challenge for the Christians — 81

**SESSION 11**
Ephesus: Compassion of the Christians                         89

**SESSION 12**
The Empty Tomb                                                97

**SESSION 13**
Christians in Pompeii                                        105

**SESSION 14**
Christians in Aphrodisias                                    113

**SESSION 15**
The Changing Face of Rome                                    119

# INTRODUCTION

# An Unexpected Transformation

At the outset of the Roman Empire, there was no Christian influence because there was no Christianity. But when Rome was at its height, the birth of a little baby in Bethlehem began to set in motion a series of events that would alter the fabric of Roman life—despite its resistance.

At the time when Jesus' earthly ministry in Israel—a part of the Roman Empire—culminated in His death by crucifixion and by His surprising resurrection, the empire was marked by worship and lifestyles that had no room for the one true God Jehovah. By its very nature, Roman culture mocked the idea that this Jesus was a king in His own right.

Not long after Jesus' resurrection, messengers and disciples who believed that Jesus was the Messiah, the Anointed One from God, began to quietly make their presence known in the empire's polytheistic society. As they went about their day-to-day existence, they endured a life of marginalization and opposition. They lived in a land where their standards of morality and their faithfulness to their Savior were either ignored or mocked, but seldom accepted.

Yet they stood their ground—not belligerently or negatively but in a way that honored Jesus' teachings such as "love your enemies" and making sure people "know them by their love."

For the most part, nations don't change overnight. Societal changes sometimes move at a glacial pace. But the Christians in Rome began to make a difference. They endured their persecution. They served their time in places like the Mamertine Prison. They practiced morality while surrounded by immorality sanctioned by the society.

And things began to change.

We look around us today, and we see Rome in reverse, we might say.

In the United States, for instance, it is rather clear that at the outset of its history, the ones who forged the land and made the laws had a basic understanding of Christianity and in many ways incorporated it into life.

Early American documents and rulings made room for God, and specific scriptural teachings were incorporated as building blocks in early laws.

Yet as US history continues to unfold, some feel that the nation is heading toward the ways of first-century Rome—where Christianity was nearly non-existent in the eyes of the government.

While the nuances of this historical argument can be debated, there is a reality that stems from a study of Christians in Rome during the early church period that is indisputable. We know that many of these brothers and sisters in Christ existed in a non-Christian world yet flourished because they obeyed scriptural teachings about living for Jesus. We can observe that no matter whether we see our society as declining or advancing in regard to matters of faith, our task—as was theirs—is to shine the light of Jesus wherever we go.

Dr. Joseph M. Stowell, the president of Cornerstone University in Grand Rapids, Michigan, and the video team from the *Day of Discovery* television program visited several locations from both the Roman Empire and the land of Israel to examine the remarkable story of how Christianity dawned upon Rome. In a study that is replete with both historical fact and biblical foundation, we are challenged by this presentation of a tiny sect of people who trusted Jesus after His resurrection, then by their life and light carried the good news of the gospel throughout a thoroughly non-believing empire.

Whether they knew it or not, these people were key to the unexpected transformation of Rome—and they can serve as a wakeup call to us that following their example just might help us transform our world as it is today, no matter where we live.

—Dave Branon
Editor

# SESSION 1

# Rome: Ruler of the World

## DAYLIGHT PREVIEW

### Touching the Past

Two thousand years after Rome ruled the known world, visitors to that great city can still touch the past. They visit the ruins of magnificent buildings—many of which were built to honor either the numerous gods of the Romans or the rulers who proclaimed themselves to be deity. Yet what most visitors to Rome may not realize is that a tiny sect of people made more magnificent contributions to the empire than even the emperors and their architects. The believers in Jesus who took Christianity to Rome not only touched the past but they also changed the future for thousands upon thousands of people throughout the land—and eventually changed the world for the better.

——————— **COME TOGETHER** ———————

*Icebreaker Questions*

1. What would you say is the greatest city you have ever visited?

2. Have you ever been to Rome? If so, what was your favorite place to visit? If not, what would you most like to visit?

3. When you were a kid, how close was history to the top of the list of your favorite subjects? Later on, how did you feel about taking "History of Western Civilization"?

 **FINDING DAYLIGHT**

### Experience the Video

Feel free to jot down Video Notes as you watch the presentation by Joe Stowell. Use the space below for those notes.

───────────── VIDEO NOTES ─────────────

Rome: *The* great city of the ancient world

Walking through the city

The Colosseum

Rome's rule

Another city: Jerusalem

Claims of a Savior

A message—and the tension it created

The message: Jesus

A threat to the Roman rulers? Hardly

Yet Christianity will conquer Rome

What led to this change?

#  WALKING IN THE DAYLIGHT

## Discussion Time

--- DISCOVER GOD'S WORD ---

*Discussion/Application Questions*

1. Why do you suppose that even though Rome fell from its height as the seat of a mighty empire some 1500 years ago, people from all around the world still stream to it?

2. What are your recollections about how Rome came to rule a massive amount of the known world?

3. What are your impressions of life in first-century Rome and elsewhere in the Roman Empire?

4. Joe Stowell states, "There was another city: Compared to the grandeur of Rome and its political muscle, relatively inconsequential—Jerusalem. Located at the end of the Mediterranean Sea, its most recent headlines were about a self-proclaimed Messiah who'd been

crucified by Rome. His followers claimed that three days after His death He rose again. They claimed to be eyewitnesses of His post-resurrection appearances. And then forty days later He ascended into heaven, promising that He would come again for them. Before He left He gave them a commission. And that was to take a simple yet clear message throughout the whole world, which would mean that it would be throughout the Roman Empire."

Read about that commission in Matthew 28:16–20.

In what way could this commission be viewed by the emperor and the leaders of the Roman Empire as a threat to their authority?

5. Read Philippians 2:1–11, a portion of the apostle Paul's letter to that first-century church within the Roman Empire.

   a. In what way could this passage be viewed by the emperor and the leaders of the Roman Empire as a threat to their authority?

   b. What kind of attitude—which Paul, in turn, was urging upon his readers—did Jesus have?

6. Joe points out that the emperors were jealously protective of their positions and powers. For them to hear that there was another king often raised a sense of paranoia and launched fierce and brutal persecution.

   How do you react to Joe's statement that if you're giving these early Christians the odds, they don't stand a chance?

7. So without sword and shield, how were Christians eventually able to "conquer" Rome, in the sense that Christianity became the state religion of the empire?

―――――――――――― BRINGING IT HOME ――――――――――――

1. What do you hope to gain from this study and from spending time with this group?

2. How do you need to grow in having the "attitude of Christ"?

## DAYLIGHT ON PRAYER

**Spending Time with God**

1. How can the group pray for your journey and relationship with God?

2. Do you have any other prayer requests to share with the group?

3. Close your prayer time by reading Philippians 2:5-11 out loud together.

## DAYLIGHT AHEAD

Fasten up, because in Session 2 you are going to cover a lot of ground. Joe Stowell will take you all the way back to the beginning—to the garden of Eden—as a reminder of God's plan for salvation. He will then take you on a history lesson to see how Rome became a world power. He'll reveal some dirty little secrets about the Roman Empire. And you will begin to see why these people needed the plan revealed way back in Adam's day.

# SESSION 2

# Rumors of a Better King

## DAYLIGHT PREVIEW

### Just What Rome Needed

History has a way of converging the paths of many stories into one huge narrative. Consider these diverse elements: The fall of mankind; the Abrahamic covenant; the rise of Alexander the Great; the ascendance of Rome. These stories converge in Rome, according to Joe Stowell, at just the right time. Christianity came to the most powerful nation in the world to meet the great needs of the people—just as God had planned it.

## COME TOGETHER

### Icebreaker Questions

1. Joe Stowell points out that Adam and Eve fell because they chose to live by their own will, saying in effect, "I will have it how I want it." According to your family (or others who knew you well), to what degree were you a "strong-willed child"?

2. How much do you enjoy watching documentaries about history or reading books about history?

3. You might be surprised as Joe talks about life for the majority of the residents of ancient Rome. What were the most crowded conditions you've lived in or temporarily experienced?

 **FINDING DAYLIGHT**

### Experience the Video

Feel free to jot down Video Notes as you watch the presentation by Joe Stowell. Use the space below for those notes.

———————————VIDEO NOTES———————————

The story of the fall

The long wait for a redeemer

God's covenant promise

Israel waited for the Messiah

18  THE DAWNING

Alexander's conquest


The Romans take over


Right time for global commission


Life in Rome


Augustus Caesar


Rumors of a better king

# WALKING IN THE DAYLIGHT

## Discussion Time

---DISCOVER GOD'S WORD---

*Discussion/Application Questions*

1. **Joe Stowell begins this session by noting that the story of the rise of Christianity in the Roman Empire actually starts at the beginning of time. Read Genesis 3:1–15.**

    a. Given the freedom to make choices, including the opportunity to enjoy God and all His creation, how do we see the heart of man saying, "I will have it how I want it"?

    b. Discuss the meaning of this: God came into the garden and called Adam and Eve back to himself.

    c. How do we see God promising that someday He would send a redeemer to restore humanity's relationship with Him, and conquer once and for all the sin and evil all of us inherit by the fall?

2. **Down the family line of Adam and Eve came Abraham, with the promise on *his* heart; and God told Abraham about His future plans for blessing the world. Read about that in Genesis 12:1–3.**

   How would God ultimately bless all peoples on earth through Abraham and his descendants?

3. **God's promise didn't end there. Read about His promise to King David, Israel's great king, in 2 Samuel 7:1–13.**

   a. What did David want to build for God?

   b. What did God promise to build for David instead?

4. **As the Jewish people waited for the coming of their promised Messiah, this King who would sit on the throne of David forever, the history of the world made some compelling turns.**

   How did Alexander the Great's massive conquest and his transportation of the Greek language and culture everywhere he went, provide the platform for both what became the Roman Empire and the rapid spread of Christianity?

5. What was surprising to you about Joe's description of daily life for the working class in first-century Rome?

6. Octavian, who lived from 63 BC to AD 14, was the first Roman emperor. He became emperor, in essence, when he defeated Mark Antony and Cleopatra at the Battle of Actium in 31 BC. The title *Augustus*, which means "exalted," was conferred upon Octavian by the Roman Senate in 27 BC. Replacing the Roman Republic with an imperial form of government, Augustus was able to incorporate the entire Mediterranean world into the empire, launch the renowned Pax Romana ("Roman Peace"), and initiate the golden age of Roman culture.

   Under Augustus Caesar, the Roman Empire achieved a new level of governmental unity, economic stability and prosperity, and infrastructure development. How did all this lend itself to what God was doing, as Paul said in Galatians 4:4, in the "fullness of time"?

7. Augustus and the emperors who followed him were not only ruthlessly violent in order to cling to their power, but they also often required the subjects of the empire to recognize the emperors as divine. In the midst of this kind of world emerged a voice that said, "There is a better King, and a better kingdom. And in it everyone matters, and there is peace for mankind."

   What would be the eventual fate of that voice, and the fate of the movement He spawned?

――――――――――― **BRINGING IT HOME** ―――――――――――

**Like Adam and Eve, we have the choice to "have it how we want it" or to enjoy God and all His creation.**

Which is better? Why?

## DAYLIGHT ON PRAYER

### Spending Time with God

1. Pray for yourself and the other members of your group to choose God's way—enjoying Him and His creation—rather than your own way.

2. What other prayer requests would you like to share with the group?

## DAYLIGHT AHEAD

While Rome was dominating the world, in faraway Israel a little baby was born who would change everything. Once Jesus' mission on earth—His death, burial, and resurrection—was made known to the people of Rome through His followers, they found themselves in a land where cruelty and state-sanctioned killings had become popular entertainment. This new faith, with its components of love and mercy, did not seem to be a perfect fit for Rome. But as Joe Stowell points out in Session 3—that is precisely why it was just the right time to take Christianity to Rome.

# SESSION 3

# Rome Resists the Gospel

 **DAYLIGHT PREVIEW**

## Fearing the Baby; Fearing the Man

We are all familiar with Herod's fear of Jesus. The Roman ruler, who had been assigned the outpost of Israel as his jurisdiction, was so fearful of this baby that he tried to have Him killed. But the opposition did not end with Herod. It continued for many years after Jesus' resurrection and ascension when His followers found their way to Rome—the home of much cruelty, as seen in the gladiatorial games. And it was in the face of much cruelty and opposition that Christians first spread the gospel, some at the cost of their lives. First, the king feared the baby, and later, the people feared the Man.

## COME TOGETHER

### Icebreaker Questions

1. Joe Stowell begins this session in Bethlehem by talking about Jesus' birth. What do you like the most—and the least—about Christmas?

2. Chariot racing was all the rage in ancient Rome. Since it was quite dangerous, auto racing might be the closest modern equivalent. How excited do you get about auto racing? Do you have a favorite driver?

3. The gladiatorial games were the other big sport in Rome. For you, what sport or athletic activity seems the closest thing to that today?

# FINDING DAYLIGHT

## Experience the Video

Feel free to jot down Video Notes as you watch the presentation by Joe Stowell. Use the space below for those notes.

———————————— VIDEO NOTES ————————————

The appointed time

Israel on the fringe

Bethlehem

Tension in Rome

26  THE DAWNING

Jesus and the disciples

Circus Maximus

Spectator sports

More cruelty was coming

Hope for believers

Heavy price to pay

Conflict between Christians and Rome

# WALKING IN THE DAYLIGHT

**Discussion Time**

---— DISCOVER GOD'S WORD ———

*Discussion/Application Questions*

1. Joe Stowell notes that God, in His "appointed time," sent His Son to be born into the midst of a bustling, powerful, pagan Roman Empire—in a stable in Bethlehem. And immediately the coming of God's Son created tension for the leaders of Rome. Read about that in Matthew 2:1–18.

   Herod, also known as Herod the Great, was the first of many rulers from his family line who were referred to as "Herod." Though not an ethnic Jew, he was appointed king of Judea by the Roman Senate in 40 BC and died shortly after Jesus was born (see Matthew 2:19).

   a. What motivated Herod to take such horrific action in Bethlehem?

   b. How much would God's plan for Jesus—and Jesus himself—be deterred by such actions?

2. How do you suppose the citizens of the Roman Empire could justify the violence, including the taking of life, that was part of the games at stadiums like the Circus Maximus?

3. Is such bloodlust totally foreign to our world today?

4. Joe notes that generally Rome was one of the most tolerant and inclusive religious empires in the history of the world.

   Why, then, did Rome see this small Jewish spin-off as a troublesome, and even potentially dangerous, sect?

5. Joe points out that nothing could be further from the truth, as the apostle Peter demonstrated in his letter to Christians who were beginning to suffer persecution. Read 1 Peter 2:13–17.

   Some Bible translations have "king" in verses 13 and 17, while others have "emperor." Peter was no doubt thinking of Nero, the emperor at the time.

   How do Peter's words speak to the perception that Christians were a threat to the empire?

6. The letter to the Hebrews, written by an unidentified author, was likely written not long after Peter wrote 1 Peter. Read Hebrews 10:32–34, a passage dealing with the readers' persecution.

   How would this public persecution actually open the hearts of people to the message of these early Christians?

7. **In the last two sessions, Joe has shared how Jesus came at just the right time in history. Read Galatians 4:4–5 with that in mind.**

   When we put together what we've learned in the last two sessions in regard to the world situation at the time of Jesus' birth and the ensuing "birth" of the church, how does it reinforce Paul's insight that "the time had fully come" (Galatians 4:4)?

---
## BRINGING IT HOME
---

**First Peter 2:13–17 tells us to submit to governing authorities, showing them honor and respect.**

How hard is it for you to have that kind of attitude toward politicians and governing authorities?

## DAYLIGHT ON PRAYER

### Spending Time with God

1. Read 1 Peter 2:17 again and pray for yourself and each other to have the attitude that this passage calls us to have toward God, fellow believers, and governing authorities.

2. Do you have any prayer requests to share with the group?

 **DAYLIGHT AHEAD**

Still in Rome, Joe Stowell visits a church to view and discuss a painting called *The Calling of St. Matthew.* As he describes the painting, he discusses Jesus' selection of people like Matthew—a hated tax collector—and he wonders why this kind of person was who Jesus wanted. And why Peter, the hot-headed impetuous one? But these are the ways of Jesus, the Man with the revolutionary way of thinking and the One who knew exactly what He was doing. There is an art lesson in Session 4—one we can all learn from.

# SESSION 4

# The Ways of Jesus

 **DAYLIGHT PREVIEW**

### Caravaggio Speaks

Think of your favorite piece of art—whether it is a painting by Monet or a stabile by Calder or a sculpture by Michelangelo or something far different—and think of analyzing its important elements. This is what Joe Stowell does in Session 4 as he visits the Church of San Luigi dei Francesi in Rome to take a closer look at *The Calling of St. Matthew* by the artist Caravaggio. Stowell discusses what this painting might reveal about some of the men Jesus called on to follow Him. And in so doing, he reveals the "ways of Jesus" as he calls it—Jesus' perhaps unorthodox methods of choosing His followers. These are the men who would be charged with taking the gospel to the ends of the earth.

―――――――――― **COME TOGETHER** ――――――――――

*Icebreaker Questions*

1. This session focuses on Matthew, who was a tax collector when Jesus called him to be one of His twelve disciples. Have you ever had any "issues" with the IRS?

2. How close to the income tax deadline do you typically get before you file your taxes?

3. A major component of this session involves a famous painting in Rome. How much of an art enthusiast are you? Do you have a favorite painting or other work of art? Do you have a favorite artist?

## FINDING DAYLIGHT

### Experience the Video

Feel free to jot down Video Notes as you watch the presentation by Joe Stowell. Use the space below for those notes.

———————————— **VIDEO NOTES** ————————————

Rome: The epicenter of the known world

The Colosseum

A painting of the calling of Matthew

Matthew, Peter, Jesus

money changing


Jesus' feet


Peter and Jesus


The ways of Jesus

## WALKING IN THE DAYLIGHT

**Discussion Time**

―――――――― **DISCOVER GOD'S WORD** ――――――――

*Discussion/Application Questions*

1. Joe Stowell speculates that for most people today the Colosseum is the most familiar image related to ancient Rome. Why do you think that is the case?

2. Many historians believe that the Colosseum, the largest amphitheater ever built in the Roman Empire, was named after a nearby hundred-foot-tall statue of Nero, called the Colossus of Nero, that Nero himself had built.

   What combined effect would these two structures—a statue of Nero ten stories tall and a massive elliptical venue capable of seating 50,000 spectators—have on visitors to Rome?

3. Next Joe visits a very different kind of site in Rome: the chapel of the Church of San Luigi dei Francesi, home of the painting entitled *The Calling of St. Matthew* by Michelangelo Merisi da Caravaggio.

   What is the significance of the fact that . . .

a. the two men on the left of the picture don't seem to notice the presence of Jesus?

b. Matthew's right hand is gripping the coins as he looks at Jesus?

c. Matthew's left hand is pointing toward himself?

d. Peter, in contrast to Matthew, is dressed in a commoner's cloak?

e. Jesus' hand is reaching out to Matthew in the same manner in which Michelangelo famously painted, on the ceiling of the Sistine Chapel, the hand of God reaching out to the hand of Adam?

f. Peter's hand is pointing toward Matthew?

4. **Now read Matthew 9:9, in which Matthew himself recounts his calling.**

   Matthew (as well as Mark and Luke, in their gospels) tells the story of his calling very matter-of-factly and succinctly. What do you make of that?

5. **Now read Matthew 9:10–13 to see what happened next.**

   As Joe points out, Jewish tax collectors were hated by the Jews. Having given their lives over to the oppressive regime of Rome to collect the exorbitant taxes, they were essentially seen as traitors. The Jews used the word "sinners" in reference to people who were notoriously evil, along with those who refused to comply with the way in which the teachers of the law applied the Law of Moses.

   a. Why would the Pharisees' disgust increase even more in light of the cultural understanding that to eat with someone was a sign of friendship?

   b. What did Jesus mean when He said, "It is not the healthy who need a doctor, but the sick"? Was He implying that the Pharisees didn't need "treatment"?

   c. What did Jesus mean when He said, "I have not come to call the righteous, but sinners"? Was He implying that the Pharisees were "righteous"?

6. Not long before Jesus called Matthew, He had already called Peter and a few other disciples. Do you think Peter's attitude toward Jesus when He called Matthew was essentially, "Who, him? You've got to be kidding—he's a tax collector"? Or do you think that Peter had learned the ways of Jesus enough to know that everybody counts, and therefore Peter welcomed Matthew with open arms?

7. Joe states that he wouldn't have chosen Matthew—or Peter. Instead, he would have gone to Jerusalem and found highly networked, wealthy people who could have really aided the cause.

    Why do you suppose Jesus didn't do that?

---------- BRINGING IT HOME ----------

Joe observes that the two men on the left of the painting *The Calling of St. Matthew* are caught up in their money changing and don't even notice the presence of Jesus, which symbolizes that in their greed they have missed an encounter with Jesus.

What is most likely to cause you to miss an encounter with Jesus?

## DAYLIGHT ON PRAYER

### Spending Time with God

1. Joe states that Caravaggio was saying, in *The Calling of St. Matthew*, that this was a compelling moment—a moment of encounter with God in which Matthew was being called to something better.

   Pray for yourself and the others in your group to have those kind of compelling moments with God, and that nothing would cause you to miss such an encounter.

2. What concerns for yourself, others, or world events would you like the group to pray about with you?

## DAYLIGHT AHEAD

We've all heard about persecution, and perhaps we have even felt the sting of being mocked or belittled for our beliefs. But sometimes it is valuable for us to be reminded of what our brothers and sisters in Christ endured in the first century as they attempted to make the gospel known and as they lived out their faith in Jesus before a world that hated them. Joe Stowell takes us to Rome to reveal some of the horrible persecution Christians suffered. From the dastardly deeds of the emperor Nero to the stark existence in the Mamertine Prison, we are exposed to man's inhumanity to man suffered by those who found Jesus worth dying for.

# SESSION 5

# Persecution of Christians

## DAYLIGHT PREVIEW

### The Fires of Hatred

By the time Nero had taken control in Rome, the gospel of Jesus Christ had begun to take hold in that city. And apparently that did not sit well with the newly crowned monarch. The stories of his persecution of Christ-followers are horrendous in their cruelty. In addition to Nero's hateful treatment of Christians, another noted source of trouble for believers was the Mamertine Prison in Rome, where notables such as Paul and Peter were incarcerated. But as we well know, the fires of hatred did not snuff out the faith—it only served to demonstrate the bravery and the faithfulness of those Jesus had called to himself.

## COME TOGETHER

### *Icebreaker Questions*

1. This session mentions the Great Fire of Rome in AD 64. What's the worst fire that you have experienced in some way?

2. Nero blamed the Christians for the fire. When you were a kid, how often did you get blamed for something you didn't do? Who usually did the blaming?

3. The focus of this session is the persecution of the early Christians. Who was the bully in your world growing up?

##  FINDING DAYLIGHT

### Experience the Video

Feel free to jot down Video Notes as you watch the presentation by Joe Stowell. Use the space below for those notes.

———————————— VIDEO NOTES ————————————

The curious lot of Christians


The only true God, miracles


The fire of Rome


Nero blamed the Christians

Corrado Primavera and Nero


Mamertine Prison


The martyrdom of Peter and Paul

## WALKING IN THE DAYLIGHT

**Discussion Time**

--- DISCOVER GOD'S WORD ---

*Discussion/Application Questions*

1. What was unique and unusual about the message of the early Christians, compared to the religions of other cultures and people groups that Rome had incorporated into the empire?

2. What words come to mind to describe Nero?

3. How seriously do you think the Roman citizens took Nero's accusation that the Christians intentionally set Rome on fire? How do you suppose the citizens felt about Nero's persecution of the Christians?

4. There is strong evidence that Paul languished in the Mamertine Prison in Rome during Nero's reign, knowing that the time of his "departure" from this life to the next was at hand (see 2 Timothy 4:6–8). According to tradition, both Paul and Peter were martyred in Rome prior to Nero's suicide in AD 68.

   Nero was the first emperor to persecute Christians. Though it isn't clear how far beyond Rome Nero's persecution spread, what effect would this outbreak have on the early Christians and their relationship with the empire?

5. The persecution of Christians accelerated again under Emperor Domitian, who ruled from AD 81 to 96. Domitian demanded to be addressed as *dominus et deus* ("lord and god"), and emperor worship became obligatory for every Roman citizen upon threat of death. The apostle John likely wrote the book of Revelation near the end of Domitian's reign. Read Revelation 2:8–11.

   Smyrna (present-day Izmir, Turkey) was strongly allied with Rome. After winning the privilege from the Roman Senate in AD 23 to build the first temple in honor of Emperor Tiberius, the residents were ready to meet the requirement of emperor worship. Adding to this, the large and hostile Jewish presence in Smyrna made life as a Christian tremendously challenging. Polycarp, bishop of Smyrna, would later become the most well-known of the early martyrs.

Jesus referred to the Christians' "poverty," caused perhaps by economic sanctions resulting from their refusal to burn a pinch of incense and proclaim Caesar as lord.

What did Christ mean, then, when He said, "Yet you are rich!"?

6. **When Jesus foretold that His followers would suffer persecution for "ten days" (v. 10), He probably meant that their tribulation would occur for a limited period of time.**

    a. What did Jesus call the believers in Smyrna to do?

    b. What did He promise them in return?

7. **Revelation 2–3 records seven messages from the risen Christ to seven churches in Asia Minor. Read Revelation 2:12–17.**

    Pergamum (present-day Bergama, Turkey) was the capital of the Roman province of Asia. The empire's first temple in honor of Augustus Caesar was built there in AD 29. As the official center of emperor worship in the province, Jesus referred to the city as "Satan's throne." According to tradition, Antipas, the first martyr of Asia, was slowly roasted to death in a bronze kettle during the reign of Domitian.

    As the one who directed the Midianites regarding how to lead the people of Israel astray (see Numbers 25:1–2; 31:16), Balaam is a fitting example of the false teachers who were leading the Christians at Pergamum to compromise with pagan society and religion. Likewise, the

Nicolaitans evidently taught that they, as Christians, could maintain a peaceful coexistence with Roman culture in general, and emperor worship in particular.

What was Christ's message to the church in Pergamum?

## BRINGING IT HOME

Though you may not face persecution—which even included the prospect of death—like many of the early Christians, what does it mean for you to be *faithful* to Christ?

## DAYLIGHT ON PRAYER

### Spending Time with God

1. How can the group pray for you in regard to growing in courage to be faithful to Christ?

2. What other requests would you like to share with the group?

# DAYLIGHT AHEAD

In Session 6, Joe Stowell will discuss something that is clearly a part of today's culture regarding Christians in western civilization: marginalization. He will tell how Romans, who misunderstood some of the things the Christians were doing, began to put the ideas of the Christian faith on the fringes of reasonable society. He begins his lesson in Rome, but then he takes an interesting side trip to Herculaneum, one of the areas that was buried under the massive volcano Vesuvius in AD 79. In both locations, Stowell reveals how outsiders can misinterpret what Christians do and believe it to be abnormal.

**SESSION 6**

# The Marginalization of Christians

## DAYLIGHT PREVIEW

### "Did You Hear What They Are Doing?"

Nobody likes to see people in their place of worship drop away—move out and away from them. Yet that's what the Christians were doing in Rome—dropping out of the synagogue to worship elsewhere. Nobody trusts people who speak in terms of having orgies or practicing cannibalism. Yet that's what non-Christian Romans thought Christians in their city were doing. Nobody wants to think a bunch of "worshipers" are neglecting the accepted deity of a society. Yet Christians were viewed as atheists because they didn't worship the temple gods. You can just hear the Roman naysayers: "Did you hear what the Christians are doing now?" Therefore, the followers of the Messiah were often marginalized and considered societal outcasts—and that makes their situation similar to what Christians experience around the world today.

## COME TOGETHER

### *Icebreaker Questions*

1. Joe Stowell notes that relationships between siblings in the Roman Empire were of absolute priority. How close were you to your siblings growing up? How about now?

2. This session looks at early Christianity's shift from gathering in Jewish synagogues to the homes of believers. How has your life been enriched by meeting with fellow Christians in smaller groups?

3. Joe mentions that sometimes he comes home and notices cars parked along the curb and wonders who's having a party. How often do you encounter that on your street? How curious do you get?

## FINDING DAYLIGHT

### Experience the Video

Feel free to jot down Video Notes as you watch the presentation by Joe Stowell. Use the space below for those notes.

———————————— VIDEO NOTES ————————————

Response of resistance

Christians in the synagogues

Example: Philippi and Lydia

Tension develops


Early church on its own


Home churches


Mount Vesuvius


Herculaneum


Rumors about Christians


Communion and cannibalism


Love feasts and orgies

Atheism

Disloyalty to emperor

Undermining the economy

Undercutting the family

Peter's message to the people of the empire

# WALKING IN THE DAYLIGHT

**Discussion Time**

--- **DISCOVER GOD'S WORD** ---

*Discussion/Application Questions*

1. Joe Stowell points out that resistance to Christianity in the Roman Empire took two basic forms. We all know about the form of persecution. But what we don't hear a lot about is another form of resistance

that was actually more pervasive, and in some respects not only more universally felt by followers of Jesus but maybe more effective.

How could marginalization be more effective than persecution?

2. Synagogues, Jewish houses of prayer, could be found throughout the Roman Empire. Since the first followers of Jesus were Jewish, they would naturally gather there. And when apostles went into a city, they would immediately go to the synagogue to tell other Jews that the Messiah had come (see Acts 14:1).

   a. Why do you think the early Christians left the synagogues and established a stand-alone religion, no longer a Jewish sect?

   b. Why do you think the shift from synagogues to individuals' homes put the early Christians more at risk and triggered more marginalization?

3. Walking the streets of Herculaneum causes Joe to imagine what it must have been like for Christians to walk down a street and enter into one of the homes. Slaves and free men, aristocrats and the poor, orphans and lame beggars would gather together for worship and fellowship.

Why would the fact that early Christianity was inclusive—that everybody was welcome—result in more resistance?

4. **Joe notes that as the followers of Jesus gathered in neighborhoods rather than synagogues they became vulnerable to the circulation of vicious, discrediting rumors.**

    What was the basis of each of the following rumors?

    a. These people are cannibals.

    b. These people are orgy-goers.

    c. These people are atheists.

    d. These people are disloyal to the emperor.

    e. These people are undermining the economy.

f. These people are undercutting the family.

5. Read what the apostle Peter wrote in 1 Peter 2:12. After that, Peter told the early Christians to submit to the governing authorities and honor the emperor.

   Now read how the apostle Paul wrote similarly in Ephesians 5:33—6:9.

   How would passages like these offset the false rumors?

## ─── BRINGING IT HOME ───

1. In what ways are Christians marginalized today?

2. To what extent do you feel that marginalization personally?

## DAYLIGHT ON PRAYER

### Spending Time with God

1. Pray that the body of Christ in general, and your church and small group in particular, would be more inclusive—even if that results in resistance or marginalization.

2. What specific prayer requests would you like to share with the group?

 ## DAYLIGHT AHEAD

From Rome, Joe Stowell journeys back to Israel—to the two little towns of Bethsaida and Capernaum—to talk about how Jesus planned to make sure His gospel was spread throughout the world. It may seem a little odd to go to those obscure villages to discuss a worldwide revolution. Yet it was from these places and others such as Tiberias and Nazareth that the message would go out. In Session 7, Joe Stowell explains how that could happen.

# SESSION 7

# The Gospel: A Traveling Enterprise

## DAYLIGHT PREVIEW

### Small-town Beginnings

You don't have to be from a big city to start a big-time enterprise. The Waltons of Bennington, Arkansas, can attest to that with their endless string of Walmarts. The New Testament tells of a major undertaking that began in not one but several small villages. Jesus headquartered in places like Capernaum and Bethsaida as He trained His disciples and headed for the cross. But He had good reason to do so, as Joe Stowell explains. Jesus could do this from humble beginnings because of the power behind the gospel—a power that not even the great city of Rome could duplicate.

## COME TOGETHER

### Icebreaker Questions

1. In this session Joe Stowell takes us to Bethsaida, a little fishing village in Galilee. What's the smallest town you've ever lived in? What are the pros and cons of living in a small town?

2. How much are you into fishing? Got any good fishing stories?

3. Joe mentions that a vast diversity of people lived in the area surrounding the Sea of Galilee. This could naturally lead to some lively discussions. How do you feel about getting into political debates? How do you feel about getting into religious debates?

 **FINDING DAYLIGHT**

## Experience the Video

Feel free to jot down Video Notes as you watch the presentation by Joe Stowell. Use the space below for those notes.

———————————— VIDEO NOTES ————————————

Power and the Christians




Bethsaida




Boys out of the hood




The charge to the disciples

Where the disciples took the gospel


What do we do with the good news?


Capernaum


The right location for conveying the message


## WALKING IN THE DAYLIGHT

**Discussion Time**

――――――― **DISCOVER GOD'S WORD** ―――――――
*Discussion/Application Questions*

1. As the early Christians walked the streets of Rome, rubbing shoulders with the soldiers who were everywhere and looking at the arches scattered all over the city celebrating the victories and conquests of the emperors, how tempting would it be for them to feel powerless?

2. What's the difference between the kind of power wielded in the plaza known as the Forum, which included the building where the Roman Senate met, and the power the early Christians possessed?

3. Joe points out that although Jesus chose most of His disciples from the fishing villages located near the Sea of Galilee, such as Bethsaida and Capernaum, they didn't stay there long-term—or even during much of Jesus' ministry, since He was an itinerate.

    Why was it important for Jesus to remove His disciples from these small towns?

4. But Joe also states that Jesus chose to headquarter His ministry in Capernaum, doing many of His miracles in or near there.

    a. What was strategic about that choice?

    b. Why didn't Jesus choose Jerusalem, or even Rome, as the center point of His ministry?

5. **After Jesus was resurrected, He gathered His disciples together and gave them a charge, saying, "You will be my witnesses in Jerusalem, and in all Judea and Samaria, and to the ends of the earth" (Acts 1:8).**

   Judea was the name of the region around Jerusalem. Samaria, home of the Samaritans (a mixed race with a partially Jewish ancestry), was the region between Judea and Galilee to the north.

   a. How do you think the disciples felt about this far-reaching commission?

   b. How well-prepared do you think they were for it?

6. **Joe notes that the disciples would indeed take the gospel to the ends of the earth as they knew it: Philip to eastern modern-day Turkey, Peter to Rome, Andrew to modern-day Istanbul, James to Spain, Thomas to India, John to Ephesus.**

   Have you typically thought of Christianity going "global" that quickly?

7. **Why is the gospel no longer the "traveling enterprise" that Jesus intended it to be?**

―――――――――――― **BRINGING IT HOME** ――――――――――――

1. Do you agree with Joe that Christians today tend to cloister the good news within the walls of our churches, essentially saying to the people around us, "Come in here and we'll tell you about Jesus"?

2. What is one step you could personally take to help move ahead in the right direction?

 **DAYLIGHT ON PRAYER**

### Spending Time with God

1. In the sense of not relying on our own knowledge, strength, and abilities, feeling "powerless" is healthy. How can the group pray for you to rely on God's power rather than your own?

2. How else can the group join you in prayer today?

**DAYLIGHT AHEAD**

Back in Capernaum, Joe Stowell visits an ancient synagogue at the location of an earlier synagogue where Jesus would have taught during His time there. Compassion is the theme of his presentation—a theme he carries with him as he discusses Jesus' great Sermon on the Mount from the location of that address. Jesus knew that persecution was coming for His followers, and He wanted them to know how to respond properly if they wanted to have an impact on the people who would be against them.

# SESSION 8

# Lessons from Capernaum

## DAYLIGHT PREVIEW

### A Call to Bless the World

What would you do if you knew that the people you were training for a mission were going to face severe opposition? Give them lessons in self-defense? Instruct them about counterattacks? Detail for them all the ways they could fight off the enemy? Here's what Jesus did: He taught His people (and by extension, us) to face opposition with compassion. He went so far as to tell them, "Love your enemies." When we are marginalized, persecuted, or even ignored because of our faith, that should be our response today as well.

## COME TOGETHER

### Icebreaker Questions

1. In this session Joe Stowell reflects on the fact that the early church was made up of all kinds of people, from the least to the greatest. What's the most diverse community or church you've ever been part of?

2. Joe notes that Jesus said His followers should be obvious as they engage their world, because they are "the light of the world." What Christ-follower have you known who is truly a shining light?

3. In the Sermon on the Mount, Jesus said that we should turn the other cheek. How hard is that for you to do?

 **FINDING DAYLIGHT**

### Experience the Video

Feel free to jot down Video Notes as you watch the presentation by Joe Stowell. Use the space below for those notes.

———————————VIDEO NOTES———————————

The Roman garrison at Capernaum

The centurion's crisis

Jesus' response

Stunning news for the Jews

Lessons for the disciples

Diversity for the kingdom

Reaching all people

Training for the disciples . . . and us

Today's Christian: Just for our kind?

Sermon on the Mount

Blessed: Persecuted

Reward? In heaven

The light of the world: Good works

Cultural engagers

# WALKING IN THE DAYLIGHT

**Discussion Time**

―――――――――― **DISCOVER GOD'S WORD** ――――――――――

*Discussion/Application Questions*

1. Why would the presence of a garrison of Roman soldiers in Capernaum be particularly irritating to the devoutly religious Jews there?

2. **The New Testament records a fascinating story about a Roman centurion. Read Luke's account of that story in Luke 7:1–10.**

   a. What was unusual about the relationship between this Roman centurion and the Jewish community?

   b. How did Jesus feel about going to the centurion's home?

   c. How did the centurion feel about Jesus coming to his home?

   d. What did Jesus find so amazing about the centurion?

3. **How did this incident serve as great training for the disciples to understand themselves and then show the Roman Empire that there was something wonderfully different about the message of Jesus Christ—namely (1) that the kingdom of God would be made up of many different kinds of people, with faith as the key; and (2) that the kingdom of God would be about reaching the rich and empowered *and* the poor and enslaved?**

4. **Next, Joe Stowell turns his attention to Jesus' famous Sermon on the Mount. Read how the sermon begins in Matthew 5:1–12.**

   a. Why is it important for Christians to realize that this isn't the only world we have—and that this world, in fact, is the short, nasty, brutish one?

   b. Why is that reality especially significant when Christians face persecution?

5. **Joe notes that after Jesus warned His disciples about the persecution they would experience for His sake—but promising them that their reward in heaven would be great—Jesus told the disciples about a strategy with which they would engage their world. Read Matthew 5:14–16.**

   What exactly is that strategy?

6. **Jesus went on to say in the Sermon on the Mount that you should turn the other cheek. Read about that in Matthew 5:38–45.**

   Joe notes that at the very beginning Jesus instructed His followers that the heart of their power would be in that they were brought into this world to bless it—no matter what—not to curse it.

a. What does Joe mean when he says that we should be *cultural engagers* rather than *cultural warriors*?

b. Which of those two terms do you think describes most Christians today? How about you?

―――――――――― BRINGING IT HOME ――――――――――

**Thinking about Jesus' compassion on a Roman centurion and a slave, and about the early Christian community being made up of all kinds of people throughout the Roman Empire—from the least to the highest— makes Joe wonder if we haven't lost something today.**

"So many of us as Christians think that Christianity is about just *our* kind of people, and that the community of faith really is about just us—with arms folded instead of arms extended."

a. If you're really honest, how much do you tend to think that Christianity is about just *our* kind of people?

b. What would it take to move your arms from *folded* to *extended*?

# DAYLIGHT ON PRAYER

## Spending Time with God

1. What personal burdens or concerns for others would you like the group to pray about with you?

2. Conclude your prayer time by asking God to help your "folded arms" to become "extended arms" and to give you a right spirit to bless and love others—even enemies.

# DAYLIGHT AHEAD

When Jesus took a trip up north with His disciples, they must have wondered why in the world He was taking them to Caesarea Philippi. This was the location of several idols of the Romans. Though it was a beautiful location at the foot of Mount Herman, it must also have been a little intimidating. But as we see in Session 9, Jesus took them there because it was a good backdrop for asking them an essential question—one that we will see Peter, who had been on hand at the Sermon on the Mount, answer correctly. And Jesus will use that answer as another reason Christians could overcome opposition.

**SESSION 9**

# The Example of Peter

## DAYLIGHT PREVIEW

### Who Am I?

What if it had been one of us who had delivered the Sermon on the Mount? Or what if it had been a person of the cloth such as your pastor? How powerful would those words have been? Would those words, presented by someone like us have been enough to cause the people of the second and third centuries to serve plague victims selflessly as Joe Stowell mentions in this session? Absolutely not. The only reason the Sermon on the Mount has power is because of the person who delivered those words. That is why Peter's declaration at Caesarea Philippi is so vital. He recognized rightly who Jesus is—that He is indeed the Messiah, the Anointed One, the Christ. That truth is at the center of any belief we have that following Jesus' words or trusting in His offer of salvation is worthwhile. "Who am I?" He asked Peter, and the mercurial disciple got it right. And so must we.

―――――――――― **COME TOGETHER** ――――――――――

*Icebreaker Questions*

1. Peter provides one of the best-known comeback stories in Scripture. What's your favorite comeback story, movie, etc.?

2. A focus of this session is the response of Christians to two devastating plagues during the era of the Roman Empire. Do you have any outstanding memories related to childhood diseases like chicken pox, measles, etc.? Who would take care of you when you got sick as a kid?

3. Name one thing you try to "avoid like the plague."

## FINDING DAYLIGHT

### Experience the Video

Feel free to jot down Video Notes as you watch the presentation by Joe Stowell. Use the space below for those notes.

———————————— VIDEO NOTES ————————————

Peter's comeback

Peter's words

The power of the kingdom: Compassion

Two plagues and Christian love

Is our world a better place because of us?

Caesarea Philippi

The location

Jesus' question

Peter's answer

Jesus' proclamation

# WALKING IN THE DAYLIGHT

## Discussion Time

### DISCOVER GOD'S WORD
*Discussion/Application Questions*

1. As Joe Stowell notes, Peter was among the crowd that listened to Jesus teach the Sermon on the Mount. Though he heard Jesus' words predicting His followers' persecution, Peter later caved in and denied Jesus. Read Mark's account of that scene in Mark 14:66–72.

   Joe goes on to say that few of the disciples became more powerful in the face of persecution and intimidation than Peter. What do you find most impressive about Peter's comeback?

2. Joe points out that the early church took the words of Jesus seriously, shining out their light in a dark world through their works of compassion and love. Joe shares the example of how the early Christians did this in the way they responded to two plagues.

   a. As people fled their villages and cities and ran into the mountains, casting their loved ones aside in the process, how could the Christians stay in the villages and cities?

b. How dramatic would the effect of their actions be upon those they rescued, and later upon their loved ones who fled and returned?

3. Do you think non-Christians today believe that our world is a better place because Christians live here? Do they see Christians more as combatants or as people of active compassion?

4. Joe recounts a story in which Jesus intentionally takes His disciples well north of Capernaum, the base of Jesus' ministry in Galilee. Read Matthew 16:13–18.

   Why would just the mention of Caesarea Philippi, according to Joe, "make any Jew worth their Torah break out into a cold sweat"?

5. Joe states that Jesus never asked a question because He didn't know the answer.

   If Jesus already knew the answers to the two questions He posed to His disciples, why did He ask them?

6. When Peter spoke up and said, "You are the Christ," what do you think he had in mind?

7. Whether or not Peter fully understood his own confession about Jesus, how would this experience at Caesarea Philippi help prepare him and the other disciples to impact the Roman Empire with its paganism and emperor worship?

───────── BRINGING IT HOME ─────────

Jesus' question to His disciples at Caesarea Philippi—"What about you? Who do you say I am?"—remains the most important question for every person to answer.

> Who do you say Jesus is? How has your understanding of Jesus and your relationship with Him progressed over time?

# DAYLIGHT ON PRAYER

## Spending Time with God

1. What prayer requests for yourself or others would you like to share with the group?

2. Pray for yourself and each other on two fronts: (1) that you would be completely committed to Jesus as "the Christ, the Son of the Living God" (Matthew 16:16); (2) that you would be people of active compassion toward those who are in need.

# DAYLIGHT AHEAD

If all you know of the city of Ephesus is what you can figure out by reading Paul's letter to the church there, Session 10 will come as a huge surprise. This city, which was a major center of commerce, was also immersed in what we can describe as an outlandish and bizarre worship pattern. At the center of town, as Joe Stowell will describe in this session, was a temple to Artemis, goddess of fertility. The details, which Stowell will provide, will indicate how difficult it must have been to live as a dedicated follower of Jesus in that community.

# SESSION 10

# Ephesus: Challenge for the Christians

## DAYLIGHT PREVIEW

### No City Limits

You have to be impressed with a first-century city that had a library with 15,000 volumes. That's a lot of scrolls! But just outside this bastion of learning and education was another building that would make today's sexual liberation-based society seem tame. It was the Temple of Artemis, and it was a beacon of immorality. Imagine living in a city in which that kind of place affected everything in the community, as Joe Stowell points out: from theater to politics to sports. Imagine also how Christians—with their God-ordained moral standards—must have been viewed in that society.

## COME TOGETHER

### Icebreaker Questions

1. The Temple of Artemis in Ephesus was one of the Seven Wonders of the Ancient World. What is the most impressive man-made "wonder" you can remember visiting?

2. Ephesus was also the home of a famous library, the third largest library in the world. When you were growing up, how much did you hang out in a library or bookmobile?

3. Tradition states that the apostle John lived in Ephesus during the latter part of his life. And since Jesus had left His mother in John's care as He suffered on the cross, Mary may have also lived out her days in Ephesus. Where would you like to live out the last of your days?

 **FINDING DAYLIGHT**

## Experience the Video

Feel free to jot down Video Notes as you watch the presentation by Joe Stowell. Use the space below for those notes.

———————————— VIDEO NOTES ————————————

The city of Ephesus

Temple of Artemis

The influence of Artemis

The challenge of the early Christians

82  THE DAWNING

Fourteen days in May

# WALKING IN THE DAYLIGHT

## Discussion Time

---DISCOVER GOD'S WORD---

*Discussion/Application Questions*

1. What reasons does Joe Stowell mention for Ephesus' status as one of the greatest cities of the ancient world?

2. What reasons does Joe mention for Ephesus' status as a significant center for early Christianity?

3. The Temple of Artemis was one of the Seven Wonders of the Ancient World. How would you describe the effect that seeing this structure—standing on a hill overlooking the city of Ephesus and gleaming in the sunlight with its marble-clad walls and 127 pillars over 60 feet high—must have had on people?

4. **Read Acts 19:8–10, in which Luke, the author of Acts, summarizes Paul's time in Ephesus.**

   Paul's ministry of two years and three months in Ephesus was the longest that the book of Acts records him staying in one missionary location. What does that say about the significance Paul placed on Ephesus and about the fruitfulness of the Lord's work there?

5. **Continue looking at Luke's account of the impact of the good news on Ephesus by reading Acts 19:11–20.**

   Joe notes that pilgrims and the citizens of Ephesus flooded into the courtyards of the Temple of Artemis because the goddess promised them healing. Specifically, pregnant women came to her, believing she held the power to protect them.

   In the Acts account, how was Christianity proving to be much greater than that?

6. **Luke now turns his focus to the riot that broke out in Ephesus. Read Acts 19:21–34.**

   Artemis was the Greek name for the Roman goddess Diana, although Artemis as seen by the Ephesians was quite different from Diana. The theater mentioned in verse 29 could seat 25,000 people, making it one of the largest outdoor theaters in the ancient world

   a. Why was Demetrius the silversmith upset?

b.  Why did the people respond like they did? What united them?

7. **Read the conclusion of this story in Acts 19:35–41.**

    The city official referred to here was the chief executive officer of the civic assembly. Though not appointed by Rome, he was the liaison between Ephesus and the Roman authorities.

    A meteorite may be the source of the claim he mentioned in verse 35 regarding an image of Artemis that supposedly had fallen from heaven.

    How was the city official able to restore order?

8. **Joe notes that the worship of Artemis included ritual prostitution and public orgies, especially during the fourteen days in May when the entire city celebrated the birthday of Artemis.**

    How challenging would it be for Christians to maintain their spiritual commitment when they would feel so terribly out of step with everything in this city?

## BRINGING IT HOME

1. How "out of step" do you feel with things in our culture?

2. How do you feel about your life in relation to the classic phrase that Christians are to be "in the world, but not of the world"?

## DAYLIGHT ON PRAYER

### Spending Time with God

1. Do you have any prayer requests to share with your group?

2. Pray for yourself and each other to have wisdom and power from God to maintain your spiritual commitment in spite of being out of step with our culture.

# DAYLIGHT AHEAD

As Joe Stowell's tour of Ephesus continues, there is more bad news—more sights and sounds of a city living on the edge of degradation. And more challenges for Christians. Sometimes their very livelihood was jeopardized by the worship of gods. Sometimes their everyday life of shopping or going to the library was tyrannized by blatant immorality. Yet, as we will see in Session 11, the Christians in this ancient city of sin found an exciting, life-giving way to demonstrate their faith to a world that needed a touch of godliness.

# SESSION 11

# Ephesus: Compassion of the Christians

## DAYLIGHT PREVIEW

### The Rescuers

Serving Jesus has a joy all its own, but imagine the absolute thrill the believers in Ephesus were able to experience as they demonstrated Christlike love in the most profound way. As you will hear from this session with Joe Stowell, they provided a service that is almost indescribable in its altruism and love: They rescued unwanted babies from the brink of death. While confused and misinformed parents were attempting to subject their newborns to an ignominious death, Christ-followers were seeking to provide them with life as a testimony to Him.

## COME TOGETHER

### *Icebreaker Questions*

1. This session begins at the Agora, the major marketplace of Ephesus, where throngs of people would have been shopping. Where is your favorite place to shop?

2. Joe Stowell notes that the silversmiths who crafted small statuettes of the goddess Artemis for visitors to take home represented one of the major industries of Ephesus. How much are you into souvenirs? What are your favorite collectibles?

3. In this session Joe focuses on the way the Christians in Ephesus showed compassion to babies. Who showed you compassion as a child?

# FINDING DAYLIGHT

## Experience the Video

Feel free to jot down Video Notes as you watch the presentation by Joe Stowell. Use the space below for those notes.

———————————— VIDEO NOTES ————————————

**The Agora: Main Street**

**Christians and the Agora**

**The shops of the Agora**

**Brothel in the neighborhood**

The sad story of the city dump


Christians to the rescue


How could this happen?


And why would Christians care?


# WALKING IN THE DAYLIGHT

**Discussion Time**

## DISCOVER GOD'S WORD
*Discussion/Application Questions*

1. Why did the Agora, the marketplace of Ephesus, represent some serious challenges for the early Christians?

2. **In the last session, we looked at the riot in Ephesus that is recorded in Acts 19. Read Acts 19:23–27 again.**

   Demetrius, no doubt, was the leader of the silversmiths who made silver shrines and statuettes of the goddess Artemis. He called together his guild, along with the guilds of related trades.

   How does this incident illustrate Joe Stowell's observation about the pressures on the early Christians and the choices they had to make as to whether they would follow Christ or be true Ephesians in the marketplace?

3. **This session takes us to the ruins of a brothel in Ephesus—the largest known brothel in the world at the time.**

   What was surprising about the location of this brothel?

4. **The backdrop of the last section of this session is the city dump of Ephesus.**

   a. How do you respond to hearing about the Roman law of death by exposure, which permitted the citizens of the empire to throw their unwanted babies away in places like the city dump of Ephesus?

   b. What reasons does Joe mention for this practice?

c. What reasons does Joe mention for the Christians rescuing these babies?

d. What effect do you think the actions of these Christians had on others?

5. As Joe says, it's really hard to imagine why people in the ancient Roman Empire would bring their babies to the city dump and leave them there to die.

    This was obviously a blind spot in their culture. Can you identify similar blind spots in our culture, particularly in regard to how "little ones" are treated?

6. What grade would you give Christians today for rescuing "little ones"—children and others who are the most vulnerable among us?

---------------- **BRINGING IT HOME** ----------------

1. **Joe notes that the early Christians lived in a world with no shame.**

   a. How similar is that to our world?

   b. How do you defend yourself from the corrupting influence of the world?

2. **Joe observes that the early Christians had learned the value of children and the value of life from Jesus, who said, "Permit the little children to come unto me," and warned that if you abuse even one of these little ones it would be better that a millstone were hung around your neck.**

   How might Jesus be compelling you to make a difference in the world in light of the value He places on children and on life?

 ## DAYLIGHT ON PRAYER

### Spending Time with God

1. What prayer concerns for yourself or others would you like to share with your group?

2. Spend some time praying silently about how you can (1) defend yourself from the corrupting influence of the world, and (2) make a difference in the world in light of the value Jesus places on children and on life.

 **DAYLIGHT AHEAD**

Sitting before the great walled city of Old Jerusalem, Joe Stowell pauses to reflect on the task that Jesus laid in the laps of His disciples. Would they be able to take His story from this city and disperse it to the world? What could possibly transform this motley crew of sometimes slow-learning men into worldwide missionaries? In Session 12 Stowell will discuss three events that will wake them up and send them out to tell the world the greatest story ever told.

# SESSION 12

# The Empty Tomb

## DAYLIGHT PREVIEW

### Twelve men; One goal

What would happen with a commercial product if the people who were charged with selling it—with making it known to the market audience—didn't believe in the product? They would have a tough time convincing others about it—and they most likely wouldn't risk their whole livelihood on it. And what would happen if just twelve men were tasked with sharing with the entire world the story of their friend's resurrection from the dead? If they weren't convinced that it was true, would they risk their lives to convey that story? Twelve men were transformed by Jesus' resurrection, and they spent the rest of their lives fulfilling the goal of spreading the good news.

## ——— COME TOGETHER ———

### *Icebreaker Questions*

1. Joe Stowell notes that Jesus had three years to prepare twelve men for global influence. What is the most intense training regimen you've experienced?

2. One of Jesus' resurrection appearances occurred at the Sea of Galilee, when discouraged Peter and his friends went back to the fishing business. What do you like to do when you're feeling down?

3. Have you ever been pegged as a "doubting Thomas"? How fitting is that label for you?

##  FINDING DAYLIGHT

### Experience the Video

Feel free to jot down Video Notes as you watch the presentation by Joe Stowell. Use the space below for those notes.

———————————— **VIDEO NOTES** ————————————

**What Jesus may have thought**




**The resurrection**




**The empty tomb**




**The appearances**

On the road to Emmaus

Together in a room

Breakfast by the sea

Announcement of the Spirit

Promise of His return

Joe's summation: Jesus is unique

# WALKING IN THE DAYLIGHT

**Discussion Time**

―――――――――――― DISCOVER GOD'S WORD ――――――――――――

*Discussion/Application Questions*

1. What do you think of Joe Stowell's speculation that there were times when Jesus wondered, because the disciples were such slow learners, if He really could trust His message to these men?

2. Joe then proceeds to say that there were two events and one promise that sealed the deal, and these things eventually made these men unstoppable.

   What were those two events and one promise?

3. Read Luke's account of Jesus' resurrection in Luke 24:1–12.

   a. Why do you suppose the disciples didn't believe the women?

   b. What do you think Peter concluded after seeing the empty tomb?

4. Jesus then appeared to two followers other than the Eleven (one named Cleopas, the other unnamed). Read Luke 24:33–49, picking up the story after these two share how Jesus revealed himself to them.

   a. What did Jesus want to impress upon His disciples?

   b. What did Jesus have planned next for them?

5. Luke wrote both the book of Acts and the gospel of Luke. Read how he begins his second book in Acts 1:1–8.

   What was the connection between the disciples' commission and their empowerment to accomplish it?

6. Now read Luke's account of Jesus' ascension in Acts 1:9–11.

   What effect did the promise of Jesus' return, in combination with His resurrection and the empowerment of the Spirit, have on the disciples?

## BRINGING IT HOME

1. **Joe acknowledges that there are times when he finds himself wondering if the message of Jesus is all that distinct.**

    "Could it be that maybe all of this is like massive superstition, just figments of our imagination, where we build these platforms to lean on in life when we can't quite do life on our own? Well, I have to say that every time I think that, my mind goes back to one very compelling reality. And that reality is that Jesus is different, that Jesus himself did something that no other religious leader did, that no god or goddess of the Roman Empire ever pulled off. And that was that He rose from the dead.

    "I feel good that there was a doubting disciple. His name was Thomas. After the resurrection of Jesus Christ, Jesus appeared to him, showed him His wounds, and then Thomas said, 'My Lord and my God!' "

    How can you relate to Joe's reflections?

2. **Read John 14:1–3, Jesus' comforting words to His disciples spoken just before He was arrested and soon thereafter crucified.**

    How does the promise of Jesus' return, in combination with His resurrection and the empowerment of the Spirit, fill your heart with resolve, courage, and confidence?

## DAYLIGHT ON PRAYER

### Spending Time with God

1. What concerns for yourself, others, or world events would you like the group to lift up in prayer?

2. Conclude your prayer time by thanking God for the resurrection of Jesus, the empowerment of the Holy Spirit, and the promise of Christ's return.

## DAYLIGHT AHEAD

In Session 13, Joe Stowell visits two places: a building in Rome that has been in continual use since the second century AD and a city in the Roman Empire that ceased to exist one horrible, fiery day in AD 79. The first is the Pantheon, an amazing edifice that was symbolic of Rome's belief in many gods. The second is Pompeii, a city whose sudden demise can make us think about the brevity of life and the importance of living for the one true God.

# SESSION 13

# Christians in Pompeii

 **DAYLIGHT PREVIEW**

### The Last Day

In both Rome and the empire's coastal city of Pompeii, August 24 in the year AD 79 began as any other. Both cities had primarily a polytheistic society with most of its citizens worshiping numerous gods while honoring the emperor as "Lord." Yet imagine if mixed in with the citizens of Pompeii were Christians: men, women, and children who were followers of Jesus and the one true God. As they went about their day on August 24, they were out of the mainstream—they walked among temples and shrines dedicated to gods they did not believe in. Suddenly, and without warning, a distant explosion rocked the city. In minutes thick ash began to fall on the people. On that day, Pompeii ceased to exist as a living city—and those who had trusted Jesus were ushered into His presence in heaven. Indeed, as Joe Stowell says in this session, it's a reminder for all of us to "number our days."

---— **COME TOGETHER** ---—

*Icebreaker Questions*

1. The eruption of Mount Vesuvius in AD 79 is highlighted in this session. Have you ever seen or visited a volcano? (If not, how about a geyser?)

2. When it comes to your temperament, are you more of a "Mount Vesuvius" or a "Lake Placid"? What would those who know you best say?

3. When Pompeii was suddenly struck with the heat of Vesuvius' eruption and buried in thick ash, life in the city was essentially frozen in time. If you could "freeze" your life in one period up to this point, what period would you choose?

# FINDING DAYLIGHT

## Experience the Video

Feel free to jot down Video Notes as you watch the presentation by Joe Stowell. Use the space below for those notes.

——————————— VIDEO NOTES ———————————

The Pantheon

Caesar worship

Immoral worship and Christians

Pompeii

Absence of the people

Christians in Pompeii

Number our days

# WALKING IN THE DAYLIGHT

## Discussion Time

### DISCOVER GOD'S WORD
*Discussion/Application Questions*

1. Joe Stowell notes that emperor worship was an effort to unify a diverse empire made up of a lot of different societal and component parts. The worship of a multiplicity of gods and Caesar was the very fabric of Roman society and also the glue of the entire political system.

   One could make the case that an act of emperor worship was more of an expression of political loyalty than of religious worship.

   a. What do you think of that notion?

   b. Since all a citizen of the empire had to do was burn a pinch of incense and say "Caesar is Lord," how tempting do you think it would be for Christians to justify such an act with an "Everybody is doing it" type of attitude?

2. Though combining sexual encounters with worshiping the gods seems incredibly foreign to us, how much pressure do you suppose the early Christians were under to conform to those practices?

3. What effect do you think it would have on you to visit Pompeii and see the plaster casts created as a result of the impressions of the bodies of Pompeii's citizens who were buried within the hardened ash that descended on their city?

4. Joe observes that Pompeii's bizarre images of Roman deities suggests something of a quiet disrespect for what the gods were about—as someone who doesn't do something *for* you, but who does something *to* you.

   How did the message of Christianity intersect with that mindset?

5. In 1 Corinthians, Paul dealt with issues relevant to these new believers' lives within their pagan culture. Read 1 Corinthians 10:14–21, where the apostle addresses idolatry in the context of the Lord's Supper.

   a. Who does Paul say that the sacrifices of the pagan Gentiles were actually being offered to?

   b. Paul later says in verse 25 that Christians didn't need to worry about the standard situation of buying meat in the public market that had been previously sacrificed to an idol. Where would Paul seem to draw the line between Christians reaching out to their pagan friends and joining them in every aspect of their lifestyle?

c. Are there modern equivalents to Paul's admonition to the early believers not to join their neighbors in participating in their pagan feasts?

6. **Now read what Paul wrote to the Corinthian believers in 1 Corinthians 6:12–20.**

How would this passage both challenge and encourage Christians to say no to the immorality associated with worshiping the gods?

---------- BRINGING IT HOME ----------

**Joe concludes this session by saying, "As I reflect on Pompeii, snuffed out in a moment of unexpected tragedy, I pause to remember what the Bible says about mankind and time. I sense how really true it is: that we would be wise to number our days and invest ourselves in things that matter, that our lifespan on earth is but a fleeting breath before a living God."**

Read Psalm 90:1–12.

a. How does this Scripture make you feel about the fleeting nature of your life?

b. How does this Scripture make you feel about the permanence of God?

c. What does it mean to you to "number your days" (v. 12)?

## DAYLIGHT ON PRAYER

### Spending Time with God

1. Do you have a prayer request to share with the group?

2. Spend some time reflecting in silence about what it means, in light of the fleeting nature of life, to number your days and invest yourself in things that matter.

# DAYLIGHT AHEAD

Who doesn't like the Olympic Games? Even if we never get a chance to actually go to London or Athens or Rio de Janeiro to see the Games in person, we can all imagine the thrill of being there. In Session 14, Joe Stowell visits an ancient stadium of the Roman Empire, in the city of Aphrodiasias, to relive the games of that city. In the sporting contests of the day, the emperor would sit in "the best seat in the house" and watch the men compete. The image of the huge crowds watching the games can remind us, Stowell says, of an important verse in Hebrews about the believer's "great cloud of witnesses," which was a vital metaphor for courage in the early church.

# SESSION 14

# Christians in Aphrodisias

## DAYLIGHT PREVIEW

### A City Like Ours?

As Joe Stowell visits city after city in the Roman Empire and describes how life was lived in the first and second centuries, a single theme continues to emerge. In religion, the people were constantly exposed to the idea that there are many gods—and for them to worship just one deity was narrow-minded. In life, the society seemed to be obsessed with sexuality and sexual freedom—even to the point that this thinking infected religion. Nineteen hundred years have passed since the time Stowell is telling us about, but has anything really changed? Does some of what he is discussing sound like what is happening where we live?

## COME TOGETHER

### *Icebreaker Questions*

1. This session takes place at the site of the ancient city of Aphrodisias, home of the renowned Temple of Aphrodite, the Greek goddess of love. Speaking of love, who was your first crush?

2. Joe Stowell notes that Aphrodisias was also home to a school of philosophy and a school of sculpturing. Which school would you be more likely to enroll in. Why?

3. Joe notes that the roar of the crowd from Aphrodisias's 30,000-seat stadium could have been heard for miles across the countryside. How excited do you get about your favorite sports team? How loudly do you cheer?

# FINDING DAYLIGHT

## Experience the Video

Feel free to jot down Video Notes as you watch the presentation by Joe Stowell. Use the space below for those notes.

———————————— VIDEO NOTES ————————————

Home of Aphrodite

Marble pillars of the temple

Early followers of Jesus in the empire

Sebastian Way

Obligation to worship gods and emperors

A different kingdom for Christians

The stadium

Running the race

A purpose for life

"City of the Cross"

## WALKING IN THE DAYLIGHT

**Discussion Time**

### ─────── DISCOVER GOD'S WORD ───────
*Discussion/Application Questions*

1. Why, according to Joe Stowell, did Augustus Caesar grant the city of Aphrodisias special tax-free privileges?

2. What was the "double pressure" the early Christians in Aphrodisias lived under?

3. What is the closest that Christians around the world today come to facing the overt pressure of emperor worship—or to the more subtle pressure of nation worship?

4. Joe draws a connection between the impressive and well-preserved stadium in Aphrodisias and a passage in the book of Hebrews. Read Hebrews 12:1–3.

    a. The "witnesses" in verse 1 are the heroes who have just been mentioned in Hebrews 11—those who had suffered for God and for God's kingdom in years and centuries past. How would they serve as more than spectators but as inspiring examples to the early Christians?

    b. Is the Christian life compared to a short sprint or a long-distance race? What are the ramifications of that difference?

    c. What does Joe mean that the Christians would envision Jesus giving them the thumbs-up sign?

5. Joe notes four elements to the early Christians' success: their compassion, their community, their sense of conviction, and their courage.

   a. How did each of these ultimately draw others to Jesus?

   b. Specifically, how would their courage both to live for and die for what they believed create a hunger in the hearts of Roman citizens for a real purpose for life?

---———————— BRINGING IT HOME ————————---

When Joe hears the words in Hebrews 12:2 about "looking unto Jesus, the author and finisher of our faith," he imagines the early Christians envisioning Jesus in the emperor's box at the stadium—that their living for Jesus was resulting in His giving them the thumbs-up sign because they're on the victory side.

   a. How could that image bolster your faith and courage not only to live for Christ but also to be willing to suffer, and even die, for Him?

   b. How would you rate your endurance in the long-distance race—the marathon—of the Christian life?

# DAYLIGHT ON PRAYER

**Spending Time with God**

1. How can the group support you in prayer as you run with endurance and perseverance the race of the Christian life?

2. What other prayer requests would you like to share with the group?

3. The change in names that accompanied Christianity coming to Aphrodisias couldn't be any more dramatic: from being named after a Greek goddess to being renamed "City of the Cross." Close your prayer time by praying for your city or community to become a "city of the cross."

# DAYLIGHT AHEAD

Standing by the famous Milvian Bridge on the outskirts of Rome, Joe Stowell takes us on one more historical journey. This one involves two warring leaders—Constantine and Maxentius—who were related by marriage but separated by differing visions for the future of Rome. Stowell explains the significance of the Battle of the Milvian Bridge—an event that would eventually lead to a huge change in how the great Roman Empire would view Christianity.

# SESSION 15

# The Changing Face of Rome

## DAYLIGHT PREVIEW

### An Extraordinary Turn of Events

Throughout these sessions, Joe Stowell has shown how marginalized Christianity was in the Roman Empire—how idol worship and immorality ruled the day. Because of their faith, Jesus' followers seemed destined for fourth-class citizenship, always relegated to the fringes of society. But remarkably, in the fourth century, Christianity became the primary faith in the land—an event that would change western civilization for the better. This remarkable story leaves us with a number of questions about how we should live in a day so similar to the pre-Christian days of Rome.

## COME TOGETHER

### *Icebreaker Questions*

1. In this session Joe Stowell recounts the Battle of the Milvian Bridge. How much interest have you had in military history? What's the most famous battlefield you've ever visited?

2. Did you play games like Risk or Battleship when you were growing up?

3. Has this series changed how you feel about studying history?

# FINDING DAYLIGHT

## Experience the Video

Feel free to jot down Video Notes as you watch the presentation by Joe Stowell. Use the space below for those notes.

———————————— VIDEO NOTES ————————————

The Milvian Bridge

AD 284: Problems in the empire

Battle of the Milvian Bridge: Constantine

Constantine goes to Rome

The Edict of Milan

Christianity becomes the formative force

Questions for us

## WALKING IN THE DAYLIGHT
**Discussion Time**

───────── DISCOVER GOD'S WORD ─────────
*Discussion/Application Questions*

1. What factors does Joe Stowell mention that led to the weakening of the Roman Empire prior to the Battle of the Milvian Bridge in AD 312?

2. The historical accounts of what Constantine experienced just before the Battle of the Milvian Bridge aren't unanimous. According to one account, he had a vision of a blazing cross in the sky and over that cross were written the words "By this sign, conquer." According to another account, Constantine had a dream in which Christ instructed

him to have his soldiers paint the first two letters of the Greek word for *Christ* on their shields.

Though people have debated both Constantine's experience before the battle and the genuineness of his self-proclaimed conversion, how likely does it seem that his motivations were entirely political in light of the fact that historians estimate that Christianity comprised no more than 10 percent of the population of the West at that time?

3. What do you make of the fact that history indicates that when Constantine entered Rome after winning the Battle of the Milvian Bridge, he didn't conclude his triumphal procession with the customary offering of pagan sacrifices?

4. Not long after that, Constantine—now the undisputed ruler of the western half of the empire—pronounced the Edict of Milan, which made Christianity a legal religion and ended all persecution against Christians. And then about 70 years later, in AD 381, the emperor Theodosius outlawed idolatry and paganism and made Christianity the sole faith of the empire, even going so far as forbidding heretics from meeting and confiscating their churches.

   a. In what way was the emperor Theodosius's decrees outlawing idolatry and paganism and making Christianity the official religion of the empire a good thing?

b. Are there ways in which his decrees might not have been such a good thing?

5. The books of the New Testament were written during a time when Christianity was by all means a minority religion. Do you think our culture today is like that, or is Christianity the majority religion of our time?

6. Joe summarizes this study by saying, "This has been the story of a man and His followers who changed their world against great odds. But it's far more than a story, certainly more than mere history. The intention is that this story be replicated in generation after generation until Jesus Christ comes back, as He promised, which means that it needs to be our story as well."

What would it mean for the story of the dawning of Christianity in the Roman Empire to become our story and for our generation to replicate that story?

## BRINGING IT HOME

1. **Joe concludes this study by asking a series of challenging questions for us as followers of Jesus Christ:**

   - Will we offer Jesus in a compelling way as did the early Christians?
   - Will we offer boundary-less communities where the broken are embraced, where the poor are welcomed and fed, and where those who need healing physically and emotionally will be supported and helped?
   - Will we offer communities that have the beautiful color of people from every tribe and nation and the richness of a diversity that is united in Jesus Christ?
   - Will we be people who have the courage and confidence of those early Christians, who believed in the power of the resurrection, and the empowerment of the indwelling Holy Spirit, and who would not be deterred regardless of the resistance?
   - Will we unashamedly proclaim the forgiving power of the cross of Jesus Christ and the life-giving power of His resurrection to help reconnect people to the God who so earnestly seeks to restore them to himself?
   - And will we seek opportunities to bless our world with acts of love and compassion, even at great risk and sacrifice to ourselves? Will we even be willing to bless those who curse us and to pray for those who may despitefully use us? In the end, will they see Jesus in us, and will we be the ones who offer them satisfaction by telling them about the indwelling person of Jesus through His finished work on the cross?

   How will you respond to this call?

2. **Finally, Joe poses this critical question for those who are still seeking:**

   What will you do with this Jesus who offers to satisfy?

   "I am the Alpha and the Omega, the Beginning and the End. I will give of the fountain of the water of life freely to him who thirsts" (Revelation 21:6).

## DAYLIGHT ON PRAYER

### Spending Time with God

1. What have you appreciated the most about this study and about this group?

2. How can the group continue to support you in prayer?

3. Conclude your prayer time by thanking God for the marvelous gift of His Son, the One who truly satisfies us.